NIGEL MANSELL

By DAVID TREMAYNE

HAZLETON PUBLISHING

PUBLISHER
Richard Poulter

EXECUTIVE PUBLISHER
Elizabeth Le Breton

ART EDITOR
Steve Small

EXECUTIVE PRODUCTION MANAGER
George Greenfield

PRODUCTION CONTROLLER
Peter Lovering

PRODUCTION ASSISTANT
Deirdre Fenney

STATISTICS
John Taylor

Colour photography by:
Front cover	–	Paul-Henri Cahier
Back cover	–	Diana Burnett
Pages 65-70, 74/5, 77, 78/9	–	David Phipps
Pages 71-74, 76	–	Paul-Henri Cahier
Page 78	–	Nigel Snowdon
Page 80	–	Diana Burnett

Black and white photographs contributed by:
Jeff Bloxham, Michael C. Brown, Peter Burn, Diana Burnett, Roger Calvert, Tony Dodgins, International Press Agency, Charles Knight, LAT, David Phipps, Duncan Raban, Keith Randall, Nigel Snowdon, Steve Swope and Ron Zuehlke.

This first edition published in 1989 by
Hazleton Publishing, 3 Richmond Hill, Richmond,
Surrey TW10 6RE.

ISBN: 0-905138-67-8

Printed in England by BAS Printers Ltd, Over Wallop, Hampshire.

Typesetting by First Impression Graphics Ltd, Richmond, Surrey.

© Hazleton Securities Ltd, 1989. No part of this publication may be reproduced, or transmitted, in any form or by any means, electronic, mechanical, photocopying, recording or otherwise, without prior permission in writing from Hazleton Securities Ltd.

DISTRIBUTOR

UK & OTHER MARKETS
Osprey Publishing Limited, 59 Grosvenor Street,
London W1X 9DA

PROLOGUE

Nobody gave the Ferrari a chance. Give it 10 laps; maybe 20. But it wouldn't last. It was a blisteringly hot 104 degrees at the Autodromo Nelson Piquet in Brazil – just what a temperamental car like the F1/89 didn't want. Mansell might be leading, but it couldn't last.

It was Sunday, 26 March 1989, and the dawn of a new era in Grand Prix racing. The Brazilian GP was the first since 1977 to run without a single turbocharged car: they had been banned at the end of 1988.

Honda Marlboro McLaren, as ever, started the race favourite, with Ayrton Senna on pole position and Alain Prost alongside Mansell on the third row of the grid. Ahead of them, Mansell's team-mate Gerhard Berger split the Williams duo, Riccardo Patrese and Thierry Boutsen. If Nigel was pondering the wisdom of leaving Williams after four years, as he watched the progress of the now Renault-engined FW12Cs in qualifying, he gave no sign of it.

At the start, he'd watched Berger dive to the left of Senna, to the inviting gap between the McLaren and Patrese's Williams. He'd seen Senna jink left, and then dart right as Berger switched to the inside line. He knew all about Ayrton's attitude. And he knew about Gerhard's, too. Neither was prepared to concede the line. As the field arrived at the first, right-hand turn, contact was inevitable.

Senna's right wheels brushed Berger's left, even though the Ferrari was halfway on the grass verge, and then Patrese ran over the McLaren's nose. Mansell could be forgiven for suppressing a smile. In 1986 he'd been on the receiving end of Senna's first-lap tactics in Rio and had come off worse against the barriers. Now it was Ayrton's turn.

The melee put him third, and two laps later he calmly picked off Boutsen. Sorry, Frank. Patrese was tougher, weaving as Mansell had known he would, but a beautiful feint to the left fooled him at the end of the straight on lap 16, and the Ferrari blasted to the right, round the outside. Four laps later he made his first pit stop, but by lap 27 he was back in the lead from Prost.

Unbeknown to him, the Frenchman's clutch had failed and he was sentenced to drive the whole distance with only two sets of tyres. Mansell, by contrast, had the luxury of a third set, which he duly called in for on lap 44. This time there was drama as he hurled his steering wheel from the cockpit. It had worked loose on its splines, and he'd radioed ahead for a replacement. But that was merely a glitch in what turned out to be a perfect afternoon.

By lap 47 he was back in the lead, and the sceptics were astonished. Surely this was the car that had broken down in three of the four practice sessions, had managed only a lap in race morning's warm-up, and which had been 'slow' all through winter testing? Hadn't Mansell himself once confided that it had an engine-wrecking tendency to shift its revolutionary semi-automatic gearbox from seventh to third down the back straight during testing at Paul Ricard? Certainly, its electro-hydraulic transmission had proved far from reliable.

Mansell himself could scarcely believe it. He'd had too many victories snatched away in the past through last-minute mechanical problems to be complacent. And two World Championships had slipped through his fingers, literally at the eleventh hour. He even admitted he was mentally assessing his chances of making an early flight home when the Ferrari went wrong.

Incredibly, it didn't. Instead it swept him home, after 61 laps, to a victory that nobody had expected, least of all the man at the wheel. But it was one he accepted gratefully. 'This is the greatest distance this car has ever done!' he beamed in disbelief. 'Up to Rio I seemed to be stuck on 13 wins, and it was getting a bit worrying. You don't know how good 14 feels!'

And if it felt good in Rio, it felt even better in Italy, where the church bells rang all night in Maranello and Modena, and the fanatical *tifosi* took him even closer to their hearts than they had when he set a record lap in his first test at their beloved Fiorano.

The Brazilian GP temporarily placed him at the top of the World Championship chase, giving him the taste of victory again after a fallow 1988. He had already admitted that Ferrari had rekindled his enthusiasm for racing, and after a long, lean spell he was a winner once more. He had consummated his new marriage with the team in the best possible way. But if his deification in Italy was remarkable, it was nothing compared to the career path that had earned him his Ferrari seat...

Mansell takes the chequered flag at Rio to win in his first race for Ferrari.

The green Lola really had no right being where it was, on the second row of the grid, fourth fastest. Formula 3 in 1977 was supposedly all about March 773s, Ralt RT1s and Chevron B38s.

Derek Warwick was on pole position by a hundredth from Stephen South, with the New Zealander, Brett Riley, next up. Nigel Mansell, two F3 races in a Puma behind him, was fourth fastest in the Lola and finished in that position after pushing South, that year's Vandervell champion, to the flag. It was an interesting pointer.

Later that October day at Silverstone came another big test. Throughout the season Mansell had fought a running battle for the Brush Fusegear Formula Ford 1600 Championship with the South African, Trevor Van Rooyen, the son of a former F1 driver. Now he faced him again for the final showdown.

Mansell had started his season in the quick but fragile Javelin and showed his pace and astonishing car control. Then he borrowed a Crossle 25F and took an impressive victory with it first time out at Thruxton. That so impressed John Crossle himself that he made a brand new 32F available to Mansell's team, which was managed by John Thornburn on behalf of sponsor Alan McKechnie.

There was one further complication. In his first race with the 32F, at Brands Hatch, a slower car put him off-line and he crashed heavily, sustaining a broken neck. The doctors said he'd be out for six months, but already the single-mindedness that would characterise his career was evident as he fought back. Only weeks later he won twice at Donington, wearing a special neck support.

By Silverstone Van Rooyen had already clinched the prestigious RAC FF1600 Championship. To pip him to the Brush Fusegear title Mansell had not only to win but, if the South African finished second, also to set fastest lap which was worth an extra point. Starting from pole position, he wrote himself into the record books with a brilliant five-second win over his rival, and fastest lap by 0.2 seconds gave him the title by a mere point.

Nigel Mansell was 23, a fully qualified hydro-mechanical engineer living in Birmingham's fashionable Hall Green. The success provided total justification for the hand-to-mouth lifestyle he and wife Rosanne had endured for the past year – but it merely whetted his appetite for more.

Born in Upton-on-Severn on 9 August 1954, he had already been competing in motorised machinery for half his life. Father Eric had done some karting, and when they visited a friend's garage in Studley one day Mansell Jnr had the

Left: *From his earliest car races, in the Hawke DL11 seen here at Mallory Park in September 1976, Nigel Mansell was to prove a fiercely competitive contender.*

The Javelin wasn't everyone's idea of a competitive FF1600, but it was in Mansell's hands. Note the loading on the left-front tyre at Silverstone in April 1977.

Below: *In the Crossle 25F borrowed from Mike 'Abacus' Taylor Nigel heads Bernard Devaney and a spinning Bernard Vermilio at Brands later that year.*

opportunity to try one of the owner's Fastakarts round the forecourt. His racing career got off to a shaky start when he damaged it badly enough to prompt its sale to his father.

Later, with a Birel 100, he soon began to make his mark. Engine failure lost him runner-up slot in the British Junior Championships in 1967, but he was invited to represent Britain in its Junior Team in Holland, and impressed. By 1968 he was a World Championship finals qualifier and travelled to Milan for the two-heat event. He was only 15, but he won the first heat with ease. When it rained for the second only the Italians had wet tyres. On slicks, he drove to a masterful eighth and third overall. Two days after his sixteenth birthday he finished second to South in the Senior class of the British Championships.

He went on to win seven Midland championships, two Welsh and a host of class awards, but by 1976 was ready to undertake a limited programme of Formula Ford 1600 races with his own Hawke DL11. In eleven events he won five and was only out of the top six twice.

By the end of 1977 the astute Thornburn, who had already helped Keke Rosberg climb the ladder, was moved to comment: 'In 19 years of motor racing, I reckon this lad has the best potential since Jimmy Clark.' Many couldn't see what he was talking about. But they would...

After throwing up a promising job with Lucas-Girling to go professional, he and Rosanne sold everything they had and moved into a tiny flat, to pay for five F3 races in 1978. Rosanne worked at the gas board, while Nigel took a job window cleaning to help keep the money coming in.

Mentor Alan McKechnie's modified Puma (right) wasn't the ideal F3 car.

Centre: *In the equally unfancied Lola T570, however, Nigel impressed here at Silverstone, the day he clinched the Brush Fusegear FF1600 crown…*

Left: *In the 32F Mansell really cemented his reputation under the auspices of Alan McKechnie. Here he leads David Leslie and a sideways Vermilio at Donington where he raced with his broken neck in a special brace after his Brands shunt.*

In the Lola again at Thruxton, where he leads Ian Flux into the chicane.

The F3 line through the chicane was obviously just as effective in FF1600. In those days Nigel raced both categories on the same day.

Fraught debut: at Donington in June 1978 his first run in an F2 car proved inconclusive and ended when he didn't qualify this ICI Chevron.

Getting in practice for later F1 life, pole-sitter Mansell (second from left) chases Derek Warwick (1) and Nelson Piquet (25) into Copse in Silverstone's F3 opener in March 1978. Jim Crawford (34) takes the wider line.

In his private March-Toyota Mansell lived up to the promise he'd shown in the Lola. A better start at Silverstone (right) takes him clear of Crawford and Michael Bleekemolen (23) in their Chevrons.

For 1979 Nigel at last secured a regular drive with the David Price-run Unipart March team, but though he could mix it with the likes of Chico Serra, Stefan Johansson and Mike Thackwell, the Triumph Dolomite engine was no match for the dominant Toyotas.

Centre: *The pressure he exerted on Andrea de Cesaris at Silverstone in March paid off when the ragged Italian missed the chicane and was penalised, thus handing Mansell his first F3 victory.*

Later that year, however, an assault by de Cesaris launched Mansell's March into a series of rolls at Oulton Park, further damaging his neck.

Mere days later, despite the pain in his damaged vertebrae, Nigel Mansell prepared for the biggest day of his life. Colin Chapman summoned him to test the Lotus 79 at Paul Ricard, where he receives counsel from team-manager Peter Collins. His strength would later save the Australian's life, at Rio in 1981.

He took pole for his first race in the works March 783, beating Warwick and Nelson Piquet, both men with whom he would spar in F1, and finished second. It was, however, an unhappy situation in which personalities failed to gel. He took another fourth and then three sevenths. And then the money ran out. Even a British Drivers' Award prize of an F2 race at Donington in June, with the ICI Chevron team, disappointed when his scheduled spare car was given, ironically enough, to his future Lotus team-mate, Elio de Angelis, and Mansell failed to qualify.

Dave Price ran the Unipart F3 team and signed him for 1979. It was the chance he so desperately needed.

The Unipart Marches ran Triumph Dolomite engines which were no match for the regular Toyotas of their rivals, but Mansell secured victory at Silverstone when Italian Andrea de Cesaris was penalised for missing out the chicane, and he showed well elsewhere too, especially at Monaco. At Silverstone for the Grand Prix meeting journalistic friend Peter Windsor made sure Colin Chapman and his assistant team-manager, Peter Collins, watched his progress as he kept ahead of a Frenchman called Alain Prost. It was to prove a crucial turning-point. Chapman went away impressed, while Collins gave him a job as engineering inspector at Lotus shortly afterwards. In the years to come he would owe Mansell his life.

Mansell's 1979 season went sour after an incident with de Cesaris at Oulton Park in September. They were chasing the Irish driver, now turned team-owner, Eddie Jordan. 'I could see something was going to happen with them as I watched in my mirrors,' Jordan recalled. 'Then on one lap de Cesaris just dived through a gap that wasn't there and I remember seeing this Unipart March rolling over and over down the road.'

Mansell's already injured neck suffered more broken vertebrae and then, only two days later, Chapman summoned him to Paul Ricard to participate in tests with South, de Angelis, Jan Lammers and Eddie Cheever. The call couldn't have come at a more inopportune moment, but it was a chance he daren't pass up.

'I went down there, taking three or four painkillers a day, but I was determined to get the test contract that was on offer. The others already had F1 experience and Stephen was going well in F2, so I thought that perhaps it wouldn't be too appetising for them. But it was an excellent opportunity for me to get in on the ground floor, and that's exactly how it turned out in the end.'

Nigel gained further experience by racing well in the F3 event at Monaco (top).

Above: F3 again was an anti-climax after the Lotus test, but at least as he chased 1980 champion-to-be Johansson round Brands he had the comfort of an F1 test contract in his pocket.

Later that year came outings in the F2 Ralt-Honda, at Silverstone (above right) and Zandvoort (right), where he was fifth. And he didn't have to pray much longer for the real F1 opportunity.

Chapman gave him the contract, and in between racing the works March 803 F3 car at the beginning of 1980, and the F2 Ralt-Honda, he tested the Lotus 81s. Within a short time he was proving his value beyond doubt.

'Every time I'd gone to Silverstone with Lotus it was for half a day or so, but then we had a two-day test in June. Things were so much better and I began to get into my rhythm.' He set the fastest-ever Lotus lap of the GP circuit, with a dramatic 1m 12.5s that had everyone sitting up and taking notice, bearing in mind that Andretti was still the number one. Using Mansell's set-up, de Angelis was later able to improve to 1m 12.1s. Later, at Brands, Nigel lopped 0.3 seconds off the Italian's previous best round the Indy circuit.

Hand in hand with the testing he was training like mad, ensuring that he stayed in peak shape ready for whenever Lotus needed him. The garage of his home in Hall Green had been converted into a gymnasium and he imposed a rigorous discipline on himself, using a combination of speedballs, weights and static bicycles. Fitness has always played a major part in his career, and he moves weights easily and confidently. While he seems trim, that appearance hides his basic strength. On one visit I tried to lift the same weights, and could barely move them off their rests...

Peter Collins had good reason to be grateful for that strength when he got into difficulties swimming off the beach outside the team's hotel in Brazil in 1981. The Australian is a strong swimmer, but suddenly found himself in trouble with the current. As his plight became obvious, Mansell swam out and performed a dramatic rescue that left Peter in his debt: 'If it hadn't been for him, helping me physically and swearing at me whenever I was tempted to give in, I wouldn't have made it.' No sooner had Mansell helped Collins to safety than he prepared to plunge back in, having heard that team-mate de Angelis was also in trouble! The Italian eventually saved himself, further down the beach – but where he and Collins were exhausted by the ordeal, Mansell remained fit and unruffled.

Nigel's pace in testing convinced Chapman that he had earned his spurs, and one day he called him to say he would be getting his Grand Prix chance in Austria. It was, after all those years, a dream come true.

The Österreichring was one of the most beautiful and challenging courses on the World Championship circuit, set in rolling hills and forests. It was fast, too, with an average lap speed of over 140 mph. Lotus took along three of its relatively unsuccessful 81s, with Mansell getting the oldest. He wasn't complaining. All

In Austria in August he finally got the chance to race the Lotus 81, and carried on until the bitter end despite sitting in a fuel bath. It was a gritty debut by any account, setting a standard he would frequently repeat.

he wanted was to do a good job, without getting in anyone's way.

He just scraped in, on the back row of the grid. He was sitting calmly, strapped into the cockpit, as the seconds ticked away before the grid was cleared for the start of the race. 'I was on a high and the old adrenalin was going, but I had to remember I had a job to do. That was very difficult with all the pressure I was feeling. But I was able to settle myself down and drive without being too distracted.'

And then, literally with only moments to go, he began to feel uncomfortable sensations. Fuel had leaked into the cockpit and he was sitting in a bath of it. Besides the obvious danger element, it was incredibly painful. 'I couldn't believe it. There I was, about to start my first GP, and I was getting the most incredible stinging pains in my backside. Everyone kept asking me if I wanted to get out, but you just don't do that when you're about to make your GP debut!'

His mechanics sloshed a gallon of water into the cockpit, and he barely had time to savour the relief before the green lights were on and he made the graduation to Grand Prix driver status. In the early laps he felt fine, held his own and began to enjoy himself. Then the water evaporated and the agony began again. In excruciating pain he willed himself on. He had every excuse to quit in the circumstances, yet he knew if he did he would lose credibility. So, lap after lap, he ground round, rising as high as 13th, ahead of Rosberg in a Fittipaldi. He was finally put out of his misery when the engine failed on lap 41.

'The decision to race was the right one; it showed I wasn't a quitter. I got a good press because of it. But the problems started when I got out of the car and discovered that my hamstrings had shrunk where they'd been immersed in petrol for so long. Afterwards I had to have them stretched.'

They were to trouble him on and off for months, but he had proved a point. He may not have been superfast – the car wasn't good enough for that, anyway – but he'd proved he was a fighter. 'I'm prepared to give 110 per cent every time I get into that car,' he told me. 'I think if you're not prepared to, you don't deserve to be there.' It was a credo he was to follow throughout his career.

He qualified and raced well at Zandvoort, but at Imola came non-qualification after he spun moving off-line for a faster car, and then watched Manfred Winkelhock crash into his stationary Lotus.

Mansell's season was over, but he had learned a lot, not least how frightening the cars of that period could be. At Imola his Lotus had porpoised violently at

While winner Carlos Reutemann's face reflects the tragic events of qualifying after the 1981 Belgian GP, and Jacques Laffite's his concern for the troubled Argentinian, Mansell celebrates his first helping of World Championship points.

At Monaco that year Nigel staggered the opposition by qualifying the new Lotus 87 an excellent third, only to retire early with suspension damage (below right).

maximum speed, as its centre of aerodynamic pressure shifted from one point to another. 'On the end of the straight the front end was literally jumping off the ground. It was porpoising so badly that my knees were being thumped at the top of the bulkhead and I had no control whatsoever over the pedals.'

It was as well that he was learning the facts of F1 life, though, because at the end of 1980 Mario Andretti quit Lotus and moved to Alfa Romeo – and Chapman looked no further than Mansell for his replacement. The hard times had finally paid off.

Within Lotus, 1981 was to prove a difficult year. Chapman began it with updated versions of the 81, the 81Bs, while preparing what should have been his next quantum leap, the 88. This remarkable vehicle had not one but two chassis, one providing ground effect, the other cocooning the driver. Mansell and de Angelis had tested the prototype 86, and then the 88, and Chapman, if not his drivers, was convinced it was a giant breakthrough. FISA was not so sure and threw it out in the season-opener at Long Beach, and again at the British GP.

All the uncertainty over the 88, and Chapman's obsession with proving its legality, detracted from the team's technical development of the single-chassis 87. Nevertheless, Mansell scored his first World Championship points with a sensational third at Zolder, where he fought successfully against Gilles Villeneuve. His performance was hailed as one of the great drives of the year. In the very next race, at Monaco, he again impressed by planting his new 87 in third spot on the grid, a tenth of a second off Nelson Piquet's pole-winning Brabham. Nigel was running third, right behind eventual victor Villeneuve, when a rear suspension link broke on lap 16. He retired, but it was the first GP in which he had run as a potential winner.

The remainder of the year failed to live up to the promise of Zolder and Monaco. The real problem, though, was the 88 saga. It reached its peak at Silverstone, where a crestfallen Mansell finally failed to qualify after beginning his meeting in an 88B and then having to scratch round after it had been hastily converted back to 87 specification. On his home ground it was a bitter pill – but his time would come.

He ended his first full season as an F1 driver with eight points thanks to a good fourth, again on a 'street' circuit, in the finale round the car park at Caesar's Palace in Las Vegas. It had been a chequered year, but he had proved a match for de Angelis on most types of circuit, and faster on the streets.

Mansell's fans wanted it, and so did Chapman, but FISA was adamant at the British GP that the Lotus 88 was not legal. Eventually he would just fail to scrape in when his car had hastily been converted back to 87 specification.

Above right: *Back in Austria he acquitted himself well in a superstars challenge event, revelling in his physical fitness. Heinz Prüller (with microphone) commentates for Austrian television.*

Right: *Three more points in Vegas rounded out a trying first season as an F1 driver.*

Right: *Teamwork: Rosanne Mansell has always been there when her husband needed a shoulder to lean on. This is Long Beach, 1982.*

How brave is brave? At Holme Pierrepont in May 1982 John Player staged this duel between a 3.5-litre V8 Velden catamaran and a 3.0-litre V8 Lotus 91. Mansell's track was narrow, bumpy and had limited stopping distance – on grass. Despite that, he pipped Bob Spalding, with 116 mph in 5.4s to the boat's 100 mph in 5.68s.

With the 88 out of Chapman's system, Mansell went forward into his second year with Lotus full of optimism. There would be a new car, the 91, and his status within the team was growing. He opened his account well with fifth in Rio, and that became third with the disqualification of Rosberg's winning Williams and Piquet's second-placed Brabham. However, 1982 developed into a black season in which badly written rules created a series of cars with rock-hard suspension. Villeneuve was killed at Zolder, and then the young Italian, Riccardo Paletti, was fatally injured at the start of the Canadian GP in Montreal.

By that stage, Mansell had finished fourth at Monaco in one of the most extraordinary races of the year, which he might well have won. Prost had led, but went into a spin in the closing stages as it began to drizzle. Then Patrese took over, only to spin. Pironi was a likely victor, but suffered electrical failure in the tunnel. Meanwhile, Daly had spun and de Cesaris had run out of fuel. If the marshals at Loews had not pushed Patrese from his 'dangerous' position, enabling him to bump-start his Brabham rolling down the hill to Portier, Mansell would have won...

Qualifying promise in Detroit turned into race day disaster and then, in Montreal, he came across Bruno Giacomelli's Alfa Romeo in the hairpin before the pits. The Italian gave no indication he intended to enter the pits, and his sudden slackening of pace caught Mansell out. As the Lotus rode over the Alfa's rear wheels Nigel's left arm became trapped in the spokes of the steering wheel. The impact was sufficient to sprain his forearm and he missed the Dutch GP that followed. A promising season was rapidly turning into a nightmare.

By 1989 Nigel Mansell's courage had become a byword in F1, but back in 1982 his plucky return to the cockpit for the British GP laid another brick in the structure of that reputation. He shouldn't really have been there at all, especially since Brands Hatch is so bumpy, and at one stage the need for swift opposite lock inflamed the wrist again during qualifying. But he kept going, determined not to miss out on his home race for the second year running. He

Trouble in store: as Derek Daly heads them into the hairpin during the Canadian GP, Mansell climbs over the back of Bruno Giacomelli's Alfa Romeo after the Italian slowed for the pits without signalling. Nigel's left wrist sustained a severe sprain when it got caught in the steering wheel during the incident.

True to form, he raced with a special cast fitted in the British GP, but over Brands Hatch's bumps he eventually had to call it a day and be helped from the cockpit.

Right: By 1983 internal pressure within Lotus, following Colin Chapman's death the previous December, saw Mansell having to make do with the Cosworth-powered 92. A moment of inspired aggression took him past Chico Serra's Arrows at Monaco's Mirabeau, as team-mate de Angelis watched in the Renault turbo-powered 93T five places further back.

Gérard Ducarouge's excellent 94T arrived just in time to boost Nigel's flagging reputation. On its debut (below right) *at Silverstone he finished a splendid fourth.*

wound up 23rd out of the 26 starters and eventually retired when the handling became too much to bear, but he *had* raced. It would be another three long years, however, before such grit was finally rewarded. Fittingly, victory would come at Brands.

All his problems paled into insignificance at the end of that year, however, when Colin Chapman died suddenly of a heart attack. The charismatic Lotus founder was the man who had given him his F1 chance, and with whom he had forged the makings of the sort of relationship Chapman had enjoyed with Jim Clark and Mario Andretti. Mansell was shattered.

'In my first months with Lotus I established a good working relationship with him. I was a bit cheeky at times, but he seemed to like that. I was always careful to be patient, not to try rushing him. He told me things to do, in confidence, and I never thought twice about doing them.' The relationship was close, and as he raced it got closer still. When he'd finished third at Zolder Chapman had doubled his retainer, and he did the same when he finished fourth at Monaco.

But beside the personal sense of loss Mansell was also to find, to his cost, that other factions at Lotus would now work against him. Peter Collins had left for Williams, and Peter Warr had returned to manage the team in 1982. He and Mansell had an uneasy relationship from the outset. Mansell felt the former Royal Horse Artillery man resented the strength of his relationship with Chapman, when he was more subordinate, while Warr thought that Mansell over-capitalised on this and began to act like a superstar after his Zolder success.

While Chapman was alive the situation merely simmered. Without him it began to assume ugly proportions. For 1983 Lotus had finally managed to jump on the ever-accelerating turbo bandwagon, through a deal with Renault. Initially, however, there would only be sufficient engines to run one car, the ungainly 93T. Warr decided that de Angelis should handle it; Mansell would have to put up with an updated Cosworth-powered 91, known as the 92, until enough Renault V6s were available. Mansell saw that as a slap in the face; Warr countered that it was logical, given de Angelis's superior results.

Either way, it scarcely mattered. The 93T was a dreadful mistake. The team called it Igor, and Mansell gave one of his most gifted performances as he braved it round Brands Hatch during the Race of Champions. It was a truly awful car. The 92 wasn't much better, giving Nigel a major fright at Imola

when the rear wing fell off at 170 mph as he approached the Tosa hairpin.

By mid-season it was the familiar Lotus story: technical confusion allied to poor reliability. The team that had dominated the 1978 World Championship looked a shadow of its former self. Appreciating the need for drastic action, Warr had signed the French designer, Gérard Ducarouge, at the beginning of June and, in a fantastic effort, the team produced two brand new 94Ts in time for the British GP at Silverstone. Mansell stormed through to fourth in his, outfoxing René Arnoux who had just dominated the Canadian GP for Ferrari.

It was another indication that, given the right equipment, Nigel Mansell possessed the ability to do the job. It seemed he now had that equipment, but the 94T flattered to deceive; his only other result was third, with fastest lap, at Brands Hatch for the GP of Europe. The vital chemistry was lacking. He'd now had three seasons with Lotus and had scored 25 World Championship points from 44 Grands Prix. His best results were three thirds. One way or another, 1984 would be his make-or-break year with the team.

Everyone makes mistakes. Mansell composes himself after a spin at Zandvoort.

In the points again: Brands Hatch 1983, GP of Europe.

Race leader: at Monaco in 1984 he shrugged off the appalling weather and was heading away from Prost and Senna when he lost it going up to Casino Square. No amount of marshal comfort (right) *could assuage the despair he felt after hitting the barriers at Massenet.*

Warr clearly wanted to replace him, and had even been making overtures to the young Brazilian, Ayrton Senna, whom Lotus would later sign and lose to McLaren, and to John Watson. John Player, however, wanted an Englishman, and so Mansell stayed for another year. Lotus had switched from the inconsistent Pirelli race tyres to Goodyears for its 95T, and the variables seemed pared to a minimum. Surely, now, Mansell had the right equipment.

The year began badly and stayed that way until the French GP at Dijon. There, under the burden of grief for the death of his mother, he raced to another third, only 24 seconds adrift of winner Niki Lauda.

At Monaco only 0.091s separated him from poleman Prost, and when the heavens opened on race day he took the lead from the Frenchman on lap 11. For five glorious laps he led, pulling away from Prost at two seconds a lap. *He wasn't just leading, he was dominating! And in such diabolical conditions!* The euphoria lasted until lap 16. Going up the hill to Massenet, by the Hotel de Paris, he got a fraction off-line, ran over the desperately slippery white line in the middle of the track, and smacked hard into the Armco barriers. The moment of glory had gone. All he could do was sit with his head in his hands.

At Dijon (left) *he was heroic, battling tooth and nail with Derek Warwick for an eventual third. Unbeknown to most, he was racing only days after the tragedy of his mother's death.*

Though he and Elio de Angelis (below) *were friendly team-mates, their relationship became a little strained after their spirited dice at Montreal in 1984* (below left).

This incident was to affect him profoundly. He just couldn't grasp the unfairness of it all. How could such a minor error have robbed him of so much? As he struggled to come to terms with it, desperation became more evident in his driving. He was having his best season, he was proving himself able to qualify with the likes of Prost, Rosberg and Piquet – and yet it was still all going wrong. What more did he have to do?

He fell out with de Angelis in Canada when the Italian made it very difficult to overtake, and triggered a startline shunt in Detroit when, after qualifying third, he aimed for the gap between Piquet and Prost just as it narrowed. That incident later cost him a hefty $6000 fine from FISA, and the threat of licence suspension.

The GP circus stayed in North America for a third event that year, with the one and only race at Dallas. The searing Texas heat broke up the track surface throughout qualifying, but Mansell took the first pole position of his career,

43

At Zandvoort Nigel had plenty to smile about: an excellent third and a new contract with Williams for 1985.

with de Angelis lined up alongside. They streaked into an early lead, re-enacting their Canadian duel. Warwick was a temporary thorn, just sliding into the lead before sliding out of it equally as fast. Again, Mansell led a Grand Prix, until Keke Rosberg went firmly on the attack. Mansell hung on grimly.

Then, as he scraped one of the unyielding concrete walls on lap 36, the Williams barged past into the lead. Nigel's attempts to retaliate were ruthlessly blocked, and then another brush with a wall damaged his gearbox. As the Lotus ground to a halt he clambered out and began pushing it to the line, until the heat finally rendered him unconscious. He was taken to the medical unit to recover, while Rosberg lost no time in lambasting him for holding him up for so long.

Warr snorted of 'limited capabilities' and by August had announced, amid great controversy with the Toleman team, that Ayrton Senna would be joining Lotus for the 1985 season. Mansell knew full well that the Brazilian would be partnering de Angelis.

If the slap in the face hurt, he showed precious little sign of it in Zandvoort for the Dutch GP, where he grabbed third place from his team-mate. It was the kind of solid result he needed after his traumas, and shortly afterwards it was announced he would be joining Frank Williams's team for 1985. Keke Rosberg had made it known to Frank that he wasn't delighted at the prospect, and Frank himself admitted later that he'd only regarded Mansell as a solid number two driver, capable of winning the odd race. As things were to turn out, though, he was to become rather more special than that.

In his last race for Lotus, in Portugal, Nigel had the outcome of the World Championship in his hands as he held the second place Lauda needed, and he and Rosberg again had a trial of strength as they momentarily banged wheels. Eventually Mansell lost a piston in a caliper after the brakes overheated. He had wanted to run the larger brakes that were available, but had been over-ruled by Warr. Their relationship remained troubled to the bitter end...

For all that Rosberg hadn't wanted him as a team-mate, the two forgot their differences quite quickly as the new season unfolded. And Mansell began to thrive in the greater harmony of the Canon Williams camp. He was in an environment where his basic ability was respected and nurtured, just as it had been by Chapman back in the early Lotus days.

Left: *At Monaco, he came close to refusing to drive the car in Saturday practice, after severe throttle problems in the Friday sessions. Brake maladies negated his bravery in the race.*

The year, nevertheless, started badly in Rio. Alboreto sat on pole in his Ferrari, from Rosberg, de Angelis, Senna and Mansell, and while Keke led at the start, Mansell and Alboreto made sharp contact on the run down to the first corner. The Williams was flipped momentarily into the air, crunched down and then spun on to the grass...an early retirement.

He raised his stock with a brilliant drive from the pit road to fifth in appalling rain at Estoril, where the Honda engine's peaky, narrow power band was very tricky, and he had further problems with it at Monaco, where he outqualified Rosberg after another display of abnormal bravery.

In the first session he was fifth, coping with a throttle problem that prevented the Honda V6 shutting down properly whenever he lifted off. 'It's one of the few times I'll admit to being scared in a racing car,' he said, grey faced. Rosberg, nearby, concurred. 'This place is nothing but an age test!' said the 1982 champion.

Starting from the pit lane, Mansell drove superbly in the diabolical conditions that marred the 1985 Portuguese GP. Despite his Honda engine's difficult power characteristics, he brought his Williams home fifth.

Mansell threatened not to drive the car on Saturday, if it was still misbehaving, but his apprehensions were swept away when it proved perfectly suited to the daunting track. With a brilliant lap he joined Senna on the front row, a mere 0.086s adrift. The race yielded only seventh, however, thanks to brake problems and a collision with the barriers as he tried to defend sixth from Jacques Laffite.

With Spa postponed, because the track had begun to break up, Canada netted sixth, while Detroit saw Rosberg burst through to win. For Mansell, however, 1985 was to be a dangerous summer. Caught out by the dirt in Turn Three, he slithered into the wall. Senna had earlier clipped the tyre wall, throwing it into confusion, and when Mansell struck the unshielded concrete head-on, he was momentarily concussed and severely jarred his right thumb. Both injuries, however, were nothing compared to what lay in wait for him at Paul Ricard.

The sun-bathed circuit in the south of France boasted one of F1's longest straights at that time, and Mansell was hurtling flat out towards the curved Signes section, conducting full tank tests on the second day of practice, when his left-rear Goodyear simply exploded. At 201 mph the flailing shreds of the tyre smashed the rear suspension and sliced away the rear wing, and the left-front wheel and suspension were torn off as he hit a plastic post set in concrete. The wheel, thrown back into the cockpit, struck him on the helmet.

Nigel was lifted unconscious from the wreckage and, after inspection at the track's medical centre, was rushed to hospital in Marseilles. A brain scan revealed severe concussion – his second in two weeks. He was out of the race but, in the circumstances, he was lucky to have survived. A similar incident had killed Mike Spence at Indianapolis in 1968.

He shrugged off the drama at Silverstone a fortnight later but, beneath his Arai helmet, he knew what his performance in qualifying fifth had cost him. He was bitterly disappointed, therefore, when his clutch broke after 17 laps, just as he felt his choice of Goodyear's harder race tyres was about to be vindicated. But the next time he appeared in front of his home crowd the result would be very different...

Five races separated him from that date with destiny: Nürburgring, Österreichring, Zandvoort, Monza and Spa. His sixth place in the first of these didn't herald any major change in fortune, but it was to be the start of the new beginning. The engine broke after he'd qualified second in Austria, while Holland brought another sixth. Monza gave him nothing more than fastest lap – but

Despite this moment caused by an apologetic Marc Surer in his Brabham, who didn't spot him in time, Nigel raced home to a solid second at Spa, his best F1 result. The final breakthrough wasn't far off...

that afternoon in September Nigel Mansell moved a step closer to his now-exalted status in F1. Third on the grid, he was running second when the electronic control box cut the Honda on to three cylinders and sent him scurrying into the pits for a replacement. He lost precisely two laps, but came out right behind Rosberg. He had nobody to race, yet he refused to lose heart, and fastest lap was his reward. That, and the consolation that he might well have won the race, since Rosberg dominated it until his engine expired.

There was nothing desperate about his driving now. Instead, he had matured into a reliable yet quick contender. As the Williams team honed designer Patrick Head's creation, so Mansell grew with it. He served further notice of his growing maturity by outqualifying Rosberg when the Belgian GP was finally restaged at Spa, battling with Prost and eventually chasing Senna home in second place. It was the best result of his career, after a finely judged race in which he hadn't put a wheel wrong. And he was about to make that final breakthrough.

Right: *Nigel and Rosanne Mansell are separated by a brace of Leos at Brands Hatch – singer Sayer and Chloe's younger brother.*

Brands Hatch is one of the spiritual homes of British motor sport and had already been the scene of some of Mansell's past successes in Formula Ford. For the Grand Prix of Europe he got off to a promising start by outqualifying Rosberg to line up behind Senna and Piquet. Inside position on the Brands grid does not traditionally favour those who line up on it, because of the steeper climb to the top of the first corner, Paddock Bend. Ironically, though, both Senna and Mansell, on that inside line, made superb starts as Rosberg on the shallower outer line faltered momentarily.

Senna, as hungry as ever, and at that time still the victor of only two GPs, was in uncompromising mood. Mansell's blinding start had him round the outside of the Brazilian as they sped into Paddock, but Senna calmly kept to his line, and used the road to the full, obliging the Englishman to run wide, out on the dirt. Rosberg, meanwhile, had suddenly rocketed away after his initially tardy start and slammed up to harry Senna for the lead. Piquet was third, an angry Mansell now only fourth. Yet again, it seemed, the cards had fallen badly for him.

Until lap seven Rosberg feinted this way and that in Senna's slipstream, the Brazilian weaving and diving as he exploited his Lotus's braking to the full. Confrontation was inevitable, and it came as the Finn tried to duck to the inside of the Lotus as they turned into Surtees, the left-hander leading out on to the back straight. Senna knew full well that the Williams-Honda's fearsome torque would get it out of the corner faster if the two cars were alongside, and he promptly chopped across. They made contact and Rosberg twitched into a spin. Piquet, right behind, couldn't quite avoid the Williams. His left-front wheel brushed its left rear, bending his own suspension and puncturing Rosberg's tyre. Piquet was out, but Rosberg still had a role to play.

The Finn limped back to the pits to have his tyres changed, and emerged just ahead of Senna and Mansell, who had managed to avoid the melee and had closed up again. The scene was set.

As the trio sped towards Surtees, Rosberg was running in the middle of the road. Senna, right behind, now had Mansell on his tail. Senna backed off a fraction, unsure of the Finn's next move. Then he darted for the right just as Mansell dived to his team-mate's left and into the lead.

He had led races before, but this time there was an air of assurance about him. Lap after lap Williams number five blasted round with the precision of a metronome, having pulled well clear of Senna after the Brazilian found himself

A winner at last! Nigel punches the air as he crosses the finish line to win the GP of Europe. It was an emotional triumph that brought the massive crowd to its feet.

Right: Heading for trouble: in Rio, Mansell and Senna speed into the first corner shortly before the incident that sidelined the Englishman's Williams FW11.

Below right: At Spa he made no mistake about his third victory, confirming that he would pose a major threat in the struggle for the 1986 World Championship crown. Nigel dedicated the success to his late team-mate Elio de Angelis, who had just been killed testing at Paul Ricard.

trapped behind the lapped Rosberg. The Lotus was no longer a match for either Williams, and gradually it began to dawn on the spectators: Mansell was going to win! All he had to do was keep his head, avoid making mistakes, and he was home and clear! And that was precisely what he did, storming to one of the most emotional victories in British racing history as he became the first Englishman in eight years to win a GP.

Suggestions he had passed Senna under a yellow flag, which would have been illegal, were officially disproved, but by then Nigel Mansell was too emotionally far gone to care. Everything he and Rosanne had endured in the past had been swept into oblivion by that brilliant success, and they were not the only ones with tears in their eyes as they embraced at the end of the greatest day in his life. Almost unnoticed, further down the pit road, Alain Prost was also celebrating. Fourth place after a gritty drive had finally clinched him the World Championship. He would win it the following year, too, but only after the cruellest fate had befallen his principal rival...Mansell.

That victory at Brands had a dramatic effect on Mansell. It was as if, having done it once, he had suddenly discovered the formula. South Africa proved he could handle pressure all the way. Starting from pole, he just had time to back off a fraction as leader Rosberg hit oil spilled at the end of the straight and spun. Mansell ducked round him and kept his head, even when a staggering recovery drive by the Finn brought him within seven seconds when the flag came out. Once again, Nigel Mansell had taken everything the best drivers in the world could throw at him, and won.

He led the finale in Adelaide, too, until Senna punted him off in a wild move and damaged his transmission. Furious, he left the track early and missed the sight of his team-mate's final victory for Williams. The Finn was McLaren-bound for 1986; Mansell now faced old F3 adversary Nelson Piquet as his team-mate. The two would make uneasy bedfellows.

Against a backdrop of Frank Williams's tragic accident, returning from a test session at Paul Ricard, the 1986 season polarised into a four-way battle between the two Williams drivers, Prost and Senna. Piquet won first time out on his home ground in Rio, while Mansell ended the race in the barrier on the first lap, after another controversial collision with Senna.

In both Canada (above left) and France, Nigel was in a class of his own as he won going away. On neither occasion could team-mate Piquet offer a serious challenge.

The two featured strongly again in the next round, at Jerez, in Spain's sherry region. Mansell came as close to winning as a driver ever can, without actually taking the chequered flag first. Slashing into the advantage Senna had built while he made a tyre stop, he crossed the line 0.014s adrift! It was the closest margin of victory ever recorded in a GP, and they shared an identical race time.

At Spa-Francorchamps Nigel again revealed the maturity of late '85, regulating his boost perfectly to defeat Senna roundly. It was an emotional triumph, however, which he dedicated immediately afterwards to de Angelis, who had been killed only days earlier testing for Brabham at Ricard.

Just as he had in South Africa, he backed his victory with another in Montreal. From pole he drove a beautiful race, conserving his fuel yet defeating Prost, Piquet and Rosberg in a straight fight. There was now no further doubt. Nigel Mansell was not just a winner; he had matured into a fearsome World Championship contender.

He was fast again in Detroit, but finished only fifth thanks to a brake problem which manifested itself just as he had taken the lead. That drag on his momentum proved only minor, however, for he was back on the top step of the rostrum at Ricard. Williams had gambled boldly on making two tyre stops as the canny Prost made one, and Mansell proved superbly adept at regaining the initiative from the Frenchman. Piquet, by contrast, was only third.

The scene was thus set for the Shell Oils British GP at Brands Hatch. The night before official qualifying began, Mansell was a guest at a function hosted by Cellnet, the mobile communications company. Relaxed and in good humour, he revealed another of the facets he had honed over the years as he gave a stylish speech outlining his tactics and hopes for the race. Even he, however, could not have known how fully they would be realised.

By this stage his relationship with Piquet had deteriorated. The Brazilian regarded himself as number one, yet Mansell was regularly outdriving him. As they set off on the opening lap, Mansell edged alongside his pole-winning team-mate, and then suddenly felt a driveshaft snap. But, just as he was cursing his luck, Thierry Boutsen spun at Paddock Bend and triggered an accident that injured veteran Jacques Laffite and brought out the red flags. The first start was null and void. Mansell could take over Piquet's spare car. He had a second chance.

He made the most of it, too, even though his new car wasn't properly set up. Piquet led but, bit by bit, Mansell closed as he got used to the car's characteristics.

After getting a second chance when the British GP was restarted, Mansell fought brilliantly to defeat the unhappy Piquet, using the Brazilian's spare car after his own broke a driveshaft in the first start. His fans (below right) had a clear message: Mansell had done what they wanted. But he had to be supported on the victory rostrum after driving the whole race without the benefit of a drink bottle.

The closest Nigel Mansell has got to McLaren is socialising with boss Ron Dennis, with whom he is seen at the German GP in 1986.

Right: In Hungary Mansell felt Piquet had deliberately misled him about the value of a new differential, and used it to his own advantage to win the race. The distortion of his rear tyres indicates how hard he was trying.

At Monza the boot stayed on Piquet's foot as the Brazilian caught and passed Mansell. By then Nigel believed implicitly that his team-mate was keeping secrets. On this occasion he felt Piquet's advantage lay in a superior rear wing.

When Piquet missed a gear he pounced. Both men were literally flat out, *mano a mano*, and in the end Mansell again triumphed convincingly, breaking Piquet's challenge in the closing stages. It was his best win yet, and put him firmly at the head of the championship table.

Piquet bounced back with wins in Germany and Hungary, where Mansell placed only third each time. Then, after both had retired in Austria, Nelson beat him again in Italy. The internal team problem was growing. Mansell accused Piquet of deliberately being misleading about the value of an alternative differential in Hungary and a new rear wing in Italy, and of using them to his own advantage. Piquet merely shrugged.

It was a see-saw season, and Portugal was Mansell's turn again, as he trounced Prost, Piquet and Senna. With only Mexico City and Adelaide left, his chances of the title looked strong. He was 10 points clear of Piquet, 70 to 60; but, under the complicated scoring structure of the series, drivers can only count their best 11 results from the 16 races. Up to Mexico he had scored 11 times, with a fifth place in Detroit as his lowest score. Thus, if he scored in Mexico, he would have to subtract two points for that fifth. A win would thus be worth seven not nine points, second only four, third only two, fourth only one...fifth would be valueless.

Sportingly, Nigel turned up as the surprise guest at Murray Walker's birthday party in a fashionable Mexican restaurant, a gesture that touched the popular commentator deeply, but the food in general in Central America disagreed with him. A badly upset stomach was yet further aggravation as the pressure began to mount.

At the start he fumbled for a gear and eventually got away in 18th place; at the end of a fruitless day he finished fifth, roundly blocked by Piquet. Gerhard Berger won in the Benetton, but Prost was a menacing second from Senna. The title chase would thus be a shoot-out between Mansell, the Frenchman and Piquet. On net scores he had 70 points, Prost 64 and Piquet 63. Prost would have to drop his worst result – sixth – and, in the event of a tie, the title would go to Mansell, which meant that he only had to finish third in Adelaide.

He led from the pole, then watched as Senna, Piquet and Rosberg burst past. It was early days yet, nothing to fret about. Now more mature, he wasn't throwing anything away in a rash move.

By lap 50, with 32 laps left, he was a comfortable third, behind Rosberg and Piquet, ahead of Prost. It was good enough. Six points for Piquet would give him 69. Not enough. Fourth place for Prost would give him 66. Again not

Overleaf: *So near, yet so far. With the championship title in the bag, Nigel lost the Australian GP when the left-rear Goodyear exploded at 200 mph. As Philippe Alliot corners ahead of him, Mansell struggles to bring his tricycling Williams to a safe halt. Note that the right-front wheel is well clear of the road...*

enough. His own third position would give him 72. Great. When Rosberg retired and Prost moved ahead of him to push Piquet, it still didn't matter: 72 for Piquet, 69 for Prost – still 72 for himself. There was no pressure.

A lap later his left-rear Goodyear exploded at 170 mph. Strips of rubber flailed in all directions as the Williams twitched and weaved, the deflated tyre lifting the opposite front corner in a grotesque parody of a can-can dancer. Sparks flew as the chassis bottomed and Mansell fought desperately for control. Still twitching, the Williams slid down the length of the straight – beyond it – into the escape road. On three wheels its braking was erratic but, somehow, Mansell got it back under control. The car bumped its nose lightly against the wall, and the rear wheels gave a final, defiant spin as he hit the throttle. But it was all over. It didn't register that Prost won both race and title after Piquet was called in for a precautionary tyre stop. All that mattered was that he had lost.

'I *can't* believe it,' he kept repeating. It was Monaco 1984 all over again, yet a thousand times worse. All that effort, all that success…for it to end like this. 'It took me a very long time to get over it,' he confessed.

The long walk home, with a championship lost.

Mansell did few F2 races in his career but the Ralt RH6, seen here at Silverstone in 1980, opened his links with Honda and kept his racing hand in as he tested for Lotus.

Lotus founder Colin Chapman was like a father-figure to the emergent young star and Nigel was devastated by his death.

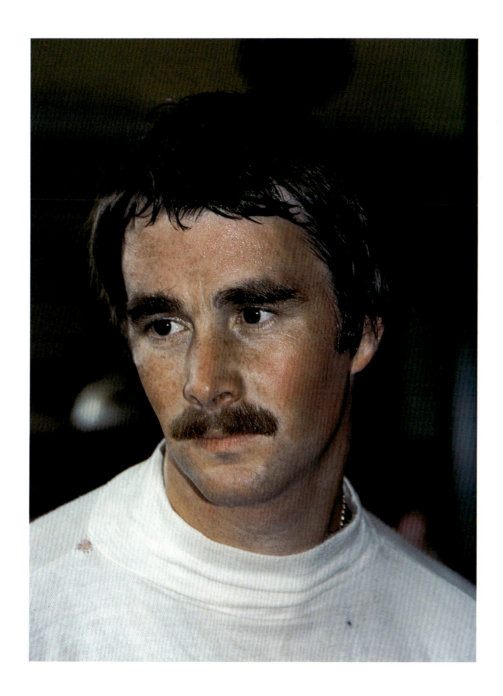

Above left: *When he had first tested the Lotus 81 at Silverstone, engineer Nigel Stroud (right) thought he was showing off, such was his speed. Before long Mansell developed a strong relationship with him and aerodynamicist Peter Wright (left).*

Left: *The great day finally came on 17 August 1980 in Austria, when Chapman offered Nigel his first Grand Prix drive. Despite – or perhaps because of – the pain from leaking fuel, he acquitted himself honourably.*

Left: Zolder in 1981 was an unhappy race, but for Mansell it brought the chance to demonstrate his latent ability with a superb third place and his first World Championship points.

Below left: Monaco 1982 was the first sign that he was a potential Grand Prix victor, but in a race that ended in turmoil he had to be satisfied with fourth.

Nigel produced a strong performance on home ground in the 1983 GP of Europe at Brands Hatch, taking third place. Here he heads Winkelhock and Tambay. The real glory days were a while off, though.

Up the hill to Massenet at Monaco in 1984, Mansell leads his first GP as he pulls away from Prost and Senna at two seconds a lap. It took him months to recover from the outcome when he skated into the barriers.

Right: At Detroit shortly afterwards he was again in blistering form, only to be accused of triggering the initial startline shunt after squeezing between Piquet and Prost on the front row.

When Nigel went to Williams for 1985 he was rated as a good number two, who might win the odd race. The coming years, however, would make him the team's most successful winner.

Right: *The sparks flew at Brands Hatch on 6 October 1985, when Nigel finally achieved the breakthrough, and that emotional maiden GP win.*

Right: Side by side with Senna, going for the line at Jerez in 1986, he came as close to winning the Spanish GP as a man could without actually taking the flag first. The Brazilian's margin of victory was an official 0.014s!

Ricard in 1987 was another copybook performance, as Mansell outclassed Piquet and outran Prost, despite two tyre-stops to the Frenchman's one.

Yet another of the retirements that influenced the outcome of the 1987 championship, as he abandons his Williams with a broken Honda engine in the German GP.

*Golfing buddies: Nigel's friendship with Australian ace
Greg Norman saw him name his second son after the
'Great White Shark'.*

*1988 was a generally barren year as he argued with
Williams over the merits of reactive ride. But, in typical
fashion, he rose brilliantly to the occasion at Silverstone
to give his home fans a treat with a fighting second.*

*Left: The effects of a bout of chickenpox forced Mansell
to pull out of the Hungarian GP after he had qualified on
the front row and held second place in the early stages.*

By his own admission, playing in the 1988 Australian Open was the most traumatic experience of his sporting career. 'At least in a car you're hidden by your helmet and face mask, and can drive away. Out there you're in the open, like it or not.'

Rio, 1989, brought that surprise victory, first time out for Ferrari. During qualifying, though, he had plenty of time to reflect on the sensitivity and unreliability of the F1/89's unique electro-hydraulic semi-automatic gearbox. This was to be one of the few occasions on which it stayed operational throughout.

Golf, whether at Long Beach (overleaf), or with Gentleman Jacques Laffite in Rio (above), had long been Nigel's passion. When he lost the championship it became a means of putting the crushing disappointment behind him, as he looked ahead to the 1987 season.

It helped that he and Rosanne could escape to the Isle of Man, to be with their children and their pets. Here was sanity, and he drew deeply on his family's emotional support as he once again immersed himself in his home life. 'Kids give you a whole different perspective on things,' he said. 'You begin to realise that some things don't matter as much as you once thought.'

He played a lot of golf, and as always he played it well. Ever since he had taken it up in 1977, when recuperating from his Brands shunt, it had relaxed him, given him a fresh interest. Predictably, like most things, he plays it to win. He once told me about his first darts game. 'I lost it, but I didn't lose another one all night! The competitive spirit is there all the time, whatever I do. And I think that's a good thing. But I can differentiate between being competitive and enjoying myself. Sometimes, if I can enjoy myself better by losing – I don't mean in racing but maybe when I'm playing table tennis or something like that – I'm happy to. I like to enjoy my life.'

By now golf had become his second major sporting love, so much so that in 1988 he would play in the Australian Open. Greg Norman was a firm friend, after whom his second son was named, but though Mansell was an impressive player, he admitted the pressure he felt was incredible.

'I'd never do another tournament until I'm much better. At one stage I was one under par, but I gripped the club so hard I hit the ball into the boonies and immediately went one over par! The pressure is amazing! And the worst thing is that you're up there, out in front of everyone, without a helmet and mask to hide behind. At least in a car you can wave fingers at the press and accelerate away, but there you're on permanent display.'

That winter he and the ever-supportive Rosanne talked Adelaide over time and again. But the detractors who thought he would now fizzle out, and come back a broken man, reckoned without his incredible determination to succeed. All Adelaide did was strengthen his resolve.

Within Williams, his relationship with Piquet was virtually non-existent, confined to nodding acquaintance. The 1986 season had built on the '85 improvement, to the point where Nigel was much more confident about himself, more prepared to follow his own route. Piquet could do what he liked. A year later the Brazilian roundly slagged off Mansell and Rosanne, and was universally chastised for it.

Overleaf: Those who expected the 1986 defeat to crush Mansell's spirit were wrong. Here he leads at Spa before his controversial clash with Senna.

Detroit (left) *should have been Nigel's, but a tyre stop and leg cramp blighted his challenge.*

At Ricard (below left) *there were no problems, just another satisfying success.*

In 1987 Mansell was more controlled than ever, and was the dominant driver of the year. He sat on pole position eight times and won six races, twice the number that Piquet managed. He won at Imola, Ricard, Silverstone (where he again pulverised Piquet in a straight fight), Österreichring, Jerez and Mexico City, and he dominated at Monaco until a broken exhaust robbed him of victory there. He should have won Spa, too, but for an extraordinary contretemps with Senna which escalated into a physical confrontation in the pits. He was also well placed in Portugal when his electrics cut out, and was walking away with Detroit until his tyre stop and Hungary before a wheel nut came loose.

The rivalry with Piquet was as strong as ever, and was not helped when Mansell thrashed him at Ricard and then repeated the dosage at Silverstone. But on those occasions when his car did break or fall back, as in Hungary, it always seemed to be the Brazilian who was there to pick up the points. Piquet's incredible consistency and a string of second places would ultimately act in his favour.

That they manifestly didn't get along is evidenced by Patrick Head's comment: 'It was a successful year as far as results were concerned, but it was painful. The loudest noise in the motorhome after a race we'd won would be the complaints of our guy who finished second.'

Piquet's softly, softly approach had reaped him 12 more points than Mansell as they headed for Suzuka and the penultimate round. During the first qualifying session the Englishman lost control entering a flat-in-fourth series of corners when he clipped a kerb with his right-front wheel. 'It didn't seem that dramatic to begin with,' he would say later. But as the left-rear wheel slid up the kerb the FW11B was thrown into a spin before slamming backwards into the tyre wall and then leaping to rest across the track. In the cockpit Mansell's face was contorted with agony as his head slumped to one side.

He suffered muscular shock and a painful battering on the base of his spine, and the doctors were adamant. There was no way he could race, not on the Sunday, nor in Adelaide. Once more, at the eleventh hour, the title had slipped from his grasp. To make things worse, the great days of Williams-Honda were at an end. In September Honda had announced its intention to supply McLaren and Lotus in 1988, after a disagreement with Williams. Mansell thus faced 1988 with a proprietary Judd V8 engine and a deteriorating relationship with the team. Said Frank: 'The trouble is, he had become the complete superstar.'

Silverstone '87: Mansell and son Leo check out the pre-race Fun Run and then driver turns photographer.

Yet again Nigel gave his home fans the result they wanted with a storming victory over team-mate Piquet.

Overleaf: *The Brazilian had his revenge next time out in Germany. Mansell led but retired with engine failure. It would have a crucial effect on his championship hopes.*

Left: *Seven years after his F1 debut there, Nigel (left) triumphed at the Österreichring after another dominant drive.*

Below left: *Monza brought another gritty battle with Piquet, but only third place at the finish behind the Brazilian and his fellow-countryman Senna.*

Below: *Congratulations! The team applaud Nigel's success in Mexico. It made up for the previous year's disappointment.*

Every picture tells a story. After his practice accident at Suzuka, Mansell's FW11B waits forlornly for its driver, bearing a message from his crew.

93

Below: *The Mansell trademark: celebratory spin-turns at the 1987 Williams Day at Brands Hatch.*

1988 proved a largely barren year as Williams adjusted to life without Honda. It wasn't until Silverstone (right) in July that Mansell finished a race, when he drove brilliantly in the rain to take second place behind Senna. As usual, his fans were delighted.

Piquet, meanwhile, was laughing all the way to the bank, a third World Championship in his pocket, won against a driver he had come to detest, and a huge multi-million dollar pay cheque awaiting him at Camel Lotus Honda.

Mansell started the season in Rio from the front row, but it was a false picture. Against the McLarens everything else was uncompetitive. The Williams FW12 was complicated by its reactive suspension system, which Mansell came to hate after a series of electronic and hydraulic failures at speed sapped his confidence. His condemnation of it brought him into conflict with Head, and harsh words frequently split the team. His best results, with standard suspension, were hard-won seconds at Silverstone and Jerez, but chickenpox contracted from daughter Chloe further blighted his year.

At the British GP he announced that he would be off to Ferrari, the greatest name in the sport. Ironically, back in 1981, he had told me: 'From the word go I always wanted to drive for Colin Chapman and Lotus. I was a fantastic fan of Jimmy Clark and basically I've never been a Ferrari man. Although one romances about it and thinks "wouldn't it be fantastic, an Englishman driving for Ferrari", I'd much rather be where I am now.' Times, however, had changed.

In 1986 he had visited Maranello for discussions about 1987. Somewhere along the line the two sides came to differing conclusions about the outcome. 'We simply discussed things and wrote them down as a memo, nothing more,' said Mansell. 'He signed a contract,' said Ferrari. There had been some threatening words from Italy, but two years on all that was forgotten.

From pacesetting in 1986 and 1987, he'd come away from 16 1988 races with a mere 12 points. Ferrari couldn't come soon enough.

Adelaide '88 marked the end of Mansell's Williams era, during which he had matured from race leader to race dominator. Sadly, his last outing was terminated by a spin after brake problems.

Above left: *Two weeks after Silverstone, the 1988 German GP was also run on a wet track, but this time Nigel's efforts resulted in retirement following this excursion onto the stadium infield.*

Left: *Mansell, team-mate Patrese and the Williams team pose for their final photo in Adelaide. Nigel's four-year spell at Didcot yielded 13 victories.*

Race driver and businessman. By 1989 the sponsorship badges (above) *had largely disappeared. At Bournemouth early in the year* (below) *Nigel outlined his new plan of attack for the season at one of the car dealerships in which he has a business interest.*

But Mansell was full of praise for Williams, the team for which he had won more races than any other driver, even though his relations with it had, in divorce parlance, 'irretrievably broken down' by the end of the season. Williams himself didn't try to hide his feelings.

'We'll miss him, no question,' said Frank of the man who had won his team 13 GPs. 'The guy is immensely quick....But I'll miss him as a driver, not as a bloke. With Alan (Jones) and Carlos (Reutemann) and Keke (Rosberg) I remember the good ups, even though we had plenty of downs. But I never felt that way with Nigel.' Aerodynamicist Frank Dernie was more gracious: 'He is a very, very quick, strong and determined driver, forceful not aggressive. He knows what he wants, and is very clever setting a car up. He's got where he is by sheer hard work and determination, but there is a natural gift in there too.' Ironically, midway through 1989 there was talk he might return to Williams for 1990...

At the beginning of 1989, in February, Mansell called a press conference for the British motor sport press. He was full of his new love affair with Ferrari and spoke emotionally of his first visit to the hallowed factory in Maranello. He hinted at the development problems the new car was going through, and he breathed large sighs of relief that he was in a position to reject sponsorship – the very sponsorship that had been so instrumental in building him his current lifestyle – because of the demands it placed on him at race meetings. 'In the past I've had up to 14 personal sponsors, all of whom required something from me at races,' he said, ingenuously. 'I've begun to realise just what pressure I've been putting on myself and I came close to overloading. Now I don't have any deals apart from with Ferrari and Marlboro. It's a great weight off my shoulders and I'm not afraid to admit it.'

It was an extraordinary remark, almost as if he regarded his past sponsors as leeches, and typified the controversy that is never far away from him. At Lotus there were the personality clashes with Warr; at Williams there was the deterioration of relationships with Frank and Patrick towards the end, both feeling he had let stardom go to his head.

The Nigel Mansell who sat before us didn't act like a superstar out of control, however. Indeed, he was to make further extraordinary remarks. He was, as he put it, 'setting out his store'. He apologised for being difficult at times in the past and promised changes. It was as if, freed from commercial obligations and again fired up with enthusiasm for racing after the reception he'd received at Ferrari, he was Born Again. It remains to be seen whether the 'newly

Right: The new start: at Rio even Nigel was surprised that the Ferrari stayed together for the entire distance to bring him his 14th victory and success in his first race for the Prancing Horse.

The trophy might have cut Mansell's fingers, but his unexpected success took him into a temporary lead in the championship and deified him in the eyes of thousands of Italians. Prost looks thoughtful, Gugelmin jubilant.

awakened' Mansell remains the type who can threaten to tear in half a photographer's picture of him sliding out of the 1984 Monaco GP, only to apologise moments later once the stress has subsided. Underneath, for sure, the same determination to succeed still burns like a magnesium fire, and as Imola and Monaco 1989 proved, when he drove his car as hard as ever despite the spectre of mechanical breakages, his abnormal bravery is still intact.

The World Championship, still his ultimate goal, has eluded him twice, yet almost because of that he is now a more complete individual. Getting over Adelaide '86 matured him immensely, even if it proved a very painful road. And Suzuka 1987 put things into focus. He still wants the championship, just as badly, but he has it in perspective. 'If it comes my way, fine. If it doesn't, okay, it's not quite the end of the world.' His real world is his family – Rosanne, Chloe, Leo and Greg – and their opulent home in Port Erin on the Isle of Man.

In Hungary last year another team's public relations man made an unfortunate joke concerning a photograph of naked men and Mansell's activities as a Special Constable. Many might have laughed it off, but Mansell didn't see the funny side of it. His police role is his contribution to the society in which he has settled, and he takes it very seriously.

In the past his stubbornness, his refusal to follow advice if he didn't feel it was right for him, has acted against him, but it is also one of the traits that has earned him his current position within F1. He is long past the stage at which he worries unduly about what people say. Now, unquestionably one of the two fastest F1 drivers in the world (the other being Senna), he styles his life the way he wants it. There are no more long-term contracts. He signs only for a year at a time, to keep himself firmly in play should expectations not be met and opportunities arise elsewhere.

At 34 he has everything apart from that world title, and has adjusted to that one shortfall. His business interests have set him up for life financially, and his 14 Grand Prix wins have moved him on to par with Sir Jack Brabham, Graham Hill and Emerson Fittipaldi. Occasionally the merry-go-round of F1 sends his reactions to certain situations spinning but, at the root, Nigel Mansell has changed little from his early racing days. There are those who say, 'In the car he's brilliant; it's a shame he ever has to get out', while others are blind in their devotion to his cause. His British fans adore him, and so, now, do the Italians. And of those who know what they are talking about, there are but a handful who don't have a towering respect for his commitment.

There are currently three drivers in F1 who can be relied upon to give 110 per cent, regardless of conditions or circumstances. Nigel Mansell, the man who parlayed a Lotus testing contract nobody rated into a regular F1 seat, and thereafter made the absolute most of it, is one of them.

Nigel's decision to race at Imola, in the wake of Berger's accident, was an act of extraordinary single-mindedness. Here the F1/89 approaches Tamburello, the fast left-hander at which his team-mate's car had earlier speared into the guard rail for reasons at that time unknown.

Right: *The Monaco GP was another stunning example of Mansell's abnormal bravery, following two narrow escapes in qualifying due to car failure. Sadly, the race brought only retirement.*

At Paul Ricard Nigel used Gerhard Berger's discarded car to race against the Austrian. More mature than ever, he finished a fine second. According to former team-mate Keke Rosberg, 'Before, Nigel was millions behind Piquet, Prost and Senna. Now that he's earning the same, he is totally relaxed, driving better than ever.'

The 1989 British Grand Prix at Silverstone saw Mansell produce yet another stirring performance in front of his devoted home fans. The Ferrari was not a match for the McLarens, but a fighting second place was further proof of Nigel's determination.

NIGEL MANSELL · CAREER RECORD
(Single seaters only)
BY JOHN TAYLOR

1976

	Race	Circuit	Date	Entrant	Car	Comment
1	FF1600 Reserve's Race	Mallory Park	29/05/76	Nigel Mansell	Hawke DL11-Ford	*Fastest lap*
1	Dunlop Star of Tomorrow FF1600 – Heat 1	Castle Combe	10/07/76	Nigel Mansell	Hawke DL11-Ford	*Fastest lap*
6	Dunlop Star of Tomorrow FF1600 – Final	Castle Combe	10/07/76	Nigel Mansell	Hawke DL11-Ford	
1	Datsun Ltd FF1600 Race	Castle Combe	12/08/76	Nigel Mansell	Hawke DL11-Ford	
1	Dunlop Star of Tomorrow FF1600 – Heat 2	Oulton Park	17/08/76	Nigel Mansell	Hawke DL11-Ford	*Fastest lap*
1	Dunlop Star of Tomorrow FF1600 – Final	Oulton Park	17/08/76	Nigel Mansell	Hawke DL11-Ford	*Fastest lap*
2	FF1600 Race	Mallory Park	19/08/76	Nigel Mansell	Hawke DL11-Ford	*Fastest lap*

1977

	Race	Circuit	Date	Entrant	Car	Comment
dns	Brush Fusegear FF1600 Race	Silverstone	06/03/77	Patrick Mulleady	Javelin JL5-Ford	*transmission in warm up/Pole*
3	Townsend-Thoresen FF1600 Race – Heat 1	Oulton Park	13/03/77	Patrick Mulleady	Javelin JL5-Ford	
3	Townsend-Thoresen FF1600 Race – Final	Oulton Park	13/03/77	Patrick Mulleady	Javelin JL5-Ford	
2	Brush Fusegear FF1600 Race – Heat 1	Silverstone	20/03/77	Patrick Mulleady	Javelin JL5-Ford	*Fastest lap*
2	Brush Fusegear FF1600 Race – Final	Silverstone	20/03/77	Patrick Mulleady	Javelin JL5-Ford	*Fastest lap*
3	Townsend-Thoresen FF1600 Race – Heat 2	Snetterton	27/03/77	Patrick Mulleady	Javelin JL5-Ford	
ret	Townsend-Thoresen FF1600 Race – Final	Snetterton	27/03/77	Patrick Mulleady	Javelin JL5-Ford	*reason unknown*
5	BARC FF1600 Race	Silverstone	03/04/77	Patrick Mulleady	Javelin JL5-Ford	
4	Townsend-Thoresen FF1600 Race	Snetterton	10/04/77	Patrick Mulleady	Javelin JL5-Ford	
2	BARC FF1600 Race	Thruxton	11/04/77	Patrick Mulleady	Javelin JL5-Ford	
1	Brush Fusegear FF1600 Race – Heat 1	Brands Hatch	01/05/77	Patrick Mulleady	Javelin JL5-Ford	*Fastest lap*
3	Brush Fusegear FF1600 Race – Final	Brands Hatch	01/05/77	Patrick Mulleady	Javelin JL5-Ford	
ret	Townsend-Thoresen FF1600 Race – Heat 2	Oulton Park	07/05/77	Patrick Mulleady	Javelin JL5-Ford	*rear suspension*
1	Brush Fusegear FF1600 Race	Thruxton	08/05/77	Alan McKechnie	Crossle 25F-Ford	*Fastest lap*
nc	Brush Fusegear FF1600 Race – Heat 2	Silverstone	15/05/77	Alan McKechnie	Crossle 25F-Ford	*1 minute penalty*
1	Brush Fusegear FF1600 Race – Heat 1	Oulton Park	22/05/77	Alan McKechnie	Crossle 25F-Ford	*Fastest lap*
ret	Brush Fusegear FF1600 Race – Final	Oulton Park	22/05/77	Alan McKechnie	Crossle 25F-Ford	*engine*
1	Townsend-Thoresen FF1600 Race – Heat 1	Brands Hatch	23/05/77	Alan McKechnie	Crossle 25F-Ford	*Fastest lap*
ret	Townsend-Thoresen FF1600 Race – Final	Brands Hatch	23/05/77	Alan McKechnie	Crossle 25F-Ford	*accident*
2	Townsend-Thoresen FF1600 Race – Heat 2	Brands Hatch	24/07/77	Alan McKechnie	Crossle 32F-Ford	*Fastest lap*
4	Townsend-Thoresen FF1600 Race – Final	Brands Hatch	24/07/77	Alan McKechnie	Crossle 32F-Ford	
1	BARC FF1600 Race – Heat 3	Donington Park	31/07/77	Alan McKechnie	Crossle 32F-Ford	*Fastest lap*
1	BARC FF1600 Race – Final	Donington Park	31/07/77	Alan McKechnie	Crossle 32F-Ford	*Fastest lap*
2	Brush Fusegear FF1600 Race – Heat 1	Donington Park	07/08/77	Alan McKechnie	Crossle 32F-Ford	
1	Brush Fusegear FF1600 Race – Final	Donington Park	07/08/77	Alan McKechnie	Crossle 32F-Ford	
3	Townsend-Thoresen FF1600 Race – Heat 1	Oulton Park	20/08/77	Alan McKechnie	Crossle 32F-Ford	
3	Townsend-Thoresen FF1600 Race – Final	Oulton Park	20/08/77	Alan McKechnie	Crossle 32F-Ford	
1	Brush Fusegear FF1600 Race – Heat 3	Mallory Park	21/08/77	Alan McKechnie	Crossle 32F-Ford	*Fastest lap*
1	Brush Fusegear FF1600 Race – Final	Mallory Park	21/08/77	Alan McKechnie	Crossle 32F-Ford	*Fastest lap*
ret	European/Vandervell F3 Race – Heat 1	Donington Park	27/08/77	Alan McKechnie	Puma 377-Toyota	*reason unknown*
1	Brush Fusegear FF1600 Race – Heat 3	Donington Park	27/08/77	Alan McKechnie	Crossle 32F-Ford	*Fastest lap*
2	Brush Fusegear FF1600 Race – Final	Donington Park	27/08/77	Alan McKechnie	Crossle 32F-Ford	*Fastest lap*
ret	Vandervell F3 Race	Silverstone	29/08/77	Alan McKechnie	Puma 377-Toyota	*reason unknown*
1	Brush Fusegear FF1600 Race – Heat 2	Silverstone	29/08/77	Alan McKechnie	Crossle 32F-Ford	*Fastest lap*
2	Brush Fusegear FF1600 Race – Final	Silverstone	29/08/77	Alan McKechnie	Crossle 32F-Ford	
1	Townsend-Thoresen FF1600 Race – Heat 1	Mallory Park	04/09/77	Alan McKechnie	Crossle 32F-Ford	*Fastest lap*
1	Townsend-Thoresen FF1600 Race – Final	Mallory Park	04/09/77	Alan McKechnie	Crossle 32F-Ford	
2	Brush Fusegear FF1600 Race – Heat 2	Donington Park	11/09/77	Alan McKechnie	Crossle 32F-Ford	*Fastest lap*
1	Brush Fusegear FF1600 Race – Final	Donington Park	11/09/77	Alan McKechnie	Crossle 32F-Ford	*Fastest lap*
2	Brush Fusegear FF1600 Race	Silverstone	18/09/77	Alan McKechnie	Crossle 32F-Ford	
1	BARC FF1600 Race – Heat 2	Oulton Park	24/09/77	Alan McKechnie	Crossle 32F-Ford	*Fastest lap*
1	BARC FF1600 Race – Final	Oulton Park	24/09/77	Alan McKechnie	Crossle 32F-Ford	*Fastest lap*
4	Vandervell F3 Race	Silverstone	01/10/77	Alan McKechnie	Lola T570-Toyota	
1	Brush Fusegear FF1600 Race	Silverstone	01/10/77	Alan McKechnie	Crossle 32F-Ford	*Fastest lap*
1	Non-Championship FF1600 Race	Donington Park	02/10/77	Alan McKechnie	Crossle 32F-Ford	*Fastest lap*
10	BP F3 Race	Thruxton	30/10/77	Alan McKechnie	Lola T570-Toyota	
1	BARC FF1600 Race	Thruxton	30/10/77	Alan McKechnie	Crossle 32F-Ford	*Fastest lap*
ret	FF1600 Festival – Heat 2	Brands Hatch	06/11/77	Alan McKechnie	Crossle 32F-Ford	*accident*
5	Non-Championship F3 Race	Thruxton	13/11/77	Alan McKechnie	Lola T570-Toyota	
1	Non-Championship FF1600 Race	Thruxton	13/11/77	Alan McKechnie	Crossle 32F-Ford	

1978

	Race	Circuit	Date	Entrant	Car	Comment
2	Vandervell F3 Race	Silverstone	19/03/78	March Engineering	March 783-Toyota	
7	BP F3 Race	Thruxton	27/03/78	March Engineering	March 783-Toyota	
7	BP F3 Race	Brands Hatch	16/04/78	March Engineering	March 783-Toyota	
7	BP F3 Race	Oulton Park	22/04/78	March Engineering	March 783-Toyota	
4	BP F3 Race	Donington Park	30/04/78	March Engineering	March 783-Toyota	
dnq	Donington '£50,000' F2 Race	Donington Park	25/06/78	Chevron Cars	Chevron B42-Hart	

1979

11	Vandervell F3 Race	Silverstone	04/03/79	Unipart Racing Team	March 783/793-Triumph	
2	Vandervell F3 Race	Thruxton	11/03/79	Unipart Racing Team	March 783/793-Triumph	
1	Vandervell F3 Race	Silverstone	25/03/79	Unipart Racing Team	March 783/793-Triumph	*1st place car disqualified*
8	Vandervell F3 Race	Snetterton	01/04/79	Unipart Racing Team	March 783/793-Triumph	
7	Vandervell F3 Race	Donington Park	08/04/79	Unipart Racing Team	March 783/793-Triumph	
4	Vandervell F3 Race	Thruxton	16/04/79	Unipart Racing Team	March 783/793-Triumph	
6	Vandervell F3 Race	Brands Hatch	07/05/79	Unipart Racing Team	March 783/793-Triumph	
6	European/Vandervell F3 Race – Heat 1	Donington Park	20/05/79	Unipart Racing Team	March 783/793-Triumph	
ret	European/Vandervell F3 Race – Final	Donington Park	20/05/79	Unipart Racing Team	March 783/793-Triumph	*accident*
11	Monaco F3 Race	Monte Carlo	26/05/79	Unipart Racing Team	March 783/793-Triumph	
4	Vandervell F3 Race	Brands Hatch	10/06/79	Unipart Racing Team	March 783/793-Triumph	
ret	Vandervell F3 Race	Cadwell Park	17/06/79	Unipart Racing Team	March 783/793-Triumph	*shock absorber/tyres*
8	Vandervell F3 Race	Silverstone	01/07/79	Unipart Racing Team	March 783/793-Triumph	
6	Vandervell F3 Race	Silverstone	14/07/79	Unipart Racing Team	March 783/793-Triumph	
6	Vandervell F3 Race	Silverstone	27/08/79	Unipart Racing Team	March 783/793-Triumph	
2	Non-Championship F3 Race	Donington Park	09/09/79	Unipart Racing Team	March 783/793-Triumph	
ret	Vandervell F3 Race	Oulton Park	15/09/79	Unipart Racing Team	March 783/793-Triumph	*accident/broken vertebrae*
8	Vandervell F3 Race	Thruxton	28/10/79	Unipart Racing Team	March 783/793-Triumph	
ret	STP Products F3 Race	Thruxton	03/11/79	Unipart Racing Team	March 783/793-Triumph	*engine*

1980

4	Vandervell F3 Race	Silverstone	02/03/80	March Engineering	March 803-Toyota	
4	Vandervell F3 Race	Thruxton	09/03/80	March Engineering	March 803-Toyota	
4	Vandervell F3 Race	Brands Hatch	30/03/80	March Engineering	March 803-Toyota	
5	Vandervell F3 Race	Thruxton	07/04/80	March Engineering	March 803-Toyota	
6	Vandervell F3 Race	Silverstone	20/04/80	March Engineering	March 803-Toyota	
ret	Vandervell F3 Race	Thruxton	06/05/80	March Engineering	March 803-Toyota	*engine*
6	Vandervell F3 Race	Snetterton	11/05/80	March Engineering	March 803-Toyota	
8	Monaco F3 Race	Monte Carlo	17/05/80	March Engineering	March 803-Toyota	
6	Vandervell F3 Race	Silverstone	26/05/80	March Engineering	March 803-Toyota	
11	Marlboro F2 Trophy	Silverstone	08/06/80	Ralt Cars Ltd	Ralt RH6-Honda	
ret	Grote Prijs van Limborg F2 Race	Zolder	22/06/80	Ralt Cars Ltd	Ralt RH6-Honda	*accident*
5	Grote Prijs van Zandvoort F2 Race	Zandvoort	20/07/80	Ralt Cars Ltd	Ralt RH6-Honda	
ret	AUSTRIAN GP	Österreichring	17/08/80	Team Essex Lotus	Lotus 81B-Cosworth DFV	*engine*
ret	DUTCH GP	Zandvoort	31/08/80	Team Essex Lotus	Lotus 81B-Cosworth DFV	*brakes/spun off*
dnq	ITALIAN GP	Imola	14/09/80	Team Essex Lotus	Lotus 81-Cosworth DFV	
2	Preis von Baden-Wurttemburg F2 Race	Hockenheim	28/09/80	Ralt Cars Ltd	Ralt RH6-Honda	

1981

10	South African Grand Prix	Kyalami	07/03/81	Team Essex Lotus	Lotus 81-Cosworth DFV	*non-championship race*
ret	US GP WEST	Long Beach	15/03/81	Team Essex Lotus	Lotus 81-Cosworth DFV	*hit wall*
11	BRAZILIAN GP	Rio	29/03/81	Team Essex Lotus	Lotus 81-Cosworth DFV	
ret	ARGENTINE GP	Buenos Aires	12/04/81	Team Essex Lotus	Lotus 81-Cosworth DFV	*engine*
3	BELGIAN GP	Zolder	17/05/81	Team Essex Lotus	Lotus 81-Cosworth DFV	
ret	MONACO GP	Monte Carlo	31/05/81	Team Essex Lotus	Lotus 87-Cosworth DFV	*rear suspension*
6	SPANISH GP	Járama	21/06/81	John Player Team Lotus	Lotus 87-Cosworth DFV	
7	FRENCH GP	Dijon	05/07/81	John Player Team Lotus	Lotus 87-Cosworth DFV	
dnq	BRITISH GP	Silverstone	18/07/81	John Player Team Lotus	Lotus 87-Cosworth DFV	
dns				John Player Team Lotus	Lotus 88B-Cosworth DFV	*disqualified during practice*
ret	GERMAN GP	Hockenheim	02/08/81	John Player Team Lotus	Lotus 87-Cosworth DFV	*fuel leak*
ret	AUSTRIAN GP	Österreichring	16/08/81	John Player Team Lotus	Lotus 87-Cosworth DFV	*engine*
ret	DUTCH GP	Zandvoort	30/08/81	John Player Team Lotus	Lotus 87-Cosworth DFV	*electrics*
ret	ITALIAN GP	Monza	13/09/81	John Player Team Lotus	Lotus 87-Cosworth DFV	*handling*
ret	CANADIAN GP	Montreal	27/09/81	John Player Team Lotus	Lotus 87-Cosworth DFV	*accident with Prost*
4	CAESAR'S PALACE GP	Las Vegas	17/10/81	John Player Team Lotus	Lotus 87-Cosworth DFV	

1982

ret	SOUTH AFRICAN GP	Kyalami	23/01/82	John Player Team Lotus	Lotus 87B-Cosworth DFV	*electrics*
3	BRAZILIAN GP	Rio	21/03/82	John Player Team Lotus	Lotus 91-Cosworth DFV	*1st and 2nd place cars disqualified*
7	US GP WEST	Long Beach	04/04/82	John Player Team Lotus	Lotus 91-Cosworth DFV	
ret	BELGIAN GP	Zolder	09/05/82	John Player Team Lotus	Lotus 91-Cosworth DFV	*clutch*
4	MONACO GP	Monte Carlo	23/05/82	John Player Team Lotus	Lotus 91-Cosworth DFV	
ret	US GP (DETROIT)	Detroit	06/06/82	John Player Team Lotus	Lotus 91-Cosworth DFV	*engine*
ret	CANADIAN GP	Montreal	13/06/82	John Player Team Lotus	Lotus 91-Cosworth DFV	*accident with Giacomelli*
ret	BRITISH GP	Brands Hatch	18/07/82	John Player Team Lotus	Lotus 91-Cosworth DFV	*handling*
9	GERMAN GP	Hockenheim	08/08/82	John Player Team Lotus	Lotus 91-Cosworth DFV	
ret	AUSTRIAN GP	Österreichring	15/08/82	John Player Team Lotus	Lotus 91-Cosworth DFV	*engine*
8	SWISS GP	Dijon	29/08/82	John Player Team Lotus	Lotus 91-Cosworth DFV	
7	ITALIAN GP	Monza	12/09/82	John Player Team Lotus	Lotus 91-Cosworth DFV	
ret	CAESAR'S PALACE GP	Las Vegas	25/09/82	John Player Team Lotus	Lotus 91-Cosworth DFV	*accident with Baldi*

1983

12	BRAZILIAN GP	Rio	13/03/83	John Player Team Lotus	Lotus 92-Cosworth DFV	
12	US GP WEST	Long Beach	27/03/83	John Player Team Lotus	Lotus 92-Cosworth DFV	
ret	Race of Champions	Brands Hatch	10/04/83	John Player Team Lotus	Lotus 93T-Renault EF1	*handling*
ret	FRENCH GP	Paul Ricard	17/04/83	John Player Team Lotus	Lotus 92-Cosworth DFV	*handling/driver discomfort*
ret	SAN MARINO GP	Imola	01/05/83	John Player Team Lotus	Lotus 92-Cosworth DFV	*broken rear wing-spun off*
ret	MONACO GP	Monte Carlo	15/05/83	John Player Team Lotus	Lotus 92-Cosworth DFV	*accident with Alboreto*
ret	BELGIAN GP	Spa	22/05/83	John Player Team Lotus	Lotus 92-Cosworth DFV	*gearbox*
6	US GP (DETROIT)	Detroit	05/06/83	John Player Team Lotus	Lotus 92-Cosworth DFV	
ret	CANADIAN GP	Montreal	12/06/83	John Player Team Lotus	Lotus 92-Cosworth DFV	*handling/tyres*
4	BRITISH GP	Silverstone	16/07/83	John Player Team Lotus	Lotus 94T-Renault EF1	
ret	GERMAN GP	Hockenheim	07/08/83	John Player Team Lotus	Lotus 94T-Renault EF1	*engine*
dns				John Player Team Lotus	Lotus 93T-Renault EF1	*practice only/grid time this car*
5	AUSTRIAN GP	Österreichring	14/08/83	John Player Team Lotus	Lotus 94T-Renault EF1	
ret	DUTCH GP	Zandvoort	28/08/83	John Player Team Lotus	Lotus 94T-Renault EF1	*spun off*
8	ITALIAN GP	Monza	11/09/83	John Player Team Lotus	Lotus 94T-Renault EF1	
3	EUROPEAN GP	Brands Hatch	25/09/83	John Player Team Lotus	Lotus 94T-Renault EF1	*Fastest lap*
nc	SOUTH AFRICAN GP	Kyalami	15/10/83	John Player Team Lotus	Lotus 94T-Renault EF1	

1984

ret	BRAZILIAN GP	Rio	25/03/84	John Player Team Lotus	Lotus 95T-Renault EF4	*slid off track*
ret	SOUTH AFRICAN GP	Kyalami	07/04/84	John Player Team Lotus	Lotus 95T-Renault EF4	*turbo inlet duct*
ret	BELGIAN GP	Zolder	29/04/84	John Player Team Lotus	Lotus 95T-Renault EF4	*clutch*
ret	SAN MARINO GP	Imola	06/05/84	John Player Team Lotus	Lotus 95T-Renault EF4	*brakes/accident*
3	FRENCH GP	Dijon	20/05/84	John Player Team Lotus	Lotus 95T-Renault EF4	
ret	MONACO GP	Monte Carlo	03/06/84	John Player Team Lotus	Lotus 95T-Renault EF4	*hit barrier when 1st*
6	CANADIAN GP	Montreal	17/06/84	John Player Team Lotus	Lotus 95T-Renault EF4	
ret	US GP (DETROIT)	Detroit	24/06/84	John Player Team Lotus	Lotus 95T-Renault EF4	*gearbox*
6/*ret*	US GP (DALLAS)	Dallas	08/07/84	John Player Team Lotus	Lotus 95T-Renault EF4	*gearbox/Pole*
ret	BRITISH GP	Brands Hatch	22/07/84	John Player Team Lotus	Lotus 95T-Renault EF4	*gearbox*
4	GERMAN GP	Hockenheim	05/08/84	John Player Team Lotus	Lotus 95T-Renault EF4	
ret	AUSTRIAN GP	Österreichring	19/08/84	John Player Team Lotus	Lotus 95T-Renault EF4	*engine*
3	DUTCH GP	Zandvoort	26/08/84	John Player Team Lotus	Lotus 95T-Renault EF4	
ret	ITALIAN GP	Monza	09/09/84	John Player Team Lotus	Lotus 95T-Renault EF4	*spun off*
ret	EUROPEAN GP	Nürburgring	07/10/84	John Player Team Lotus	Lotus 95T-Renault EF4	*engine*
ret	PORTUGUESE GP	Estoril	21/10/84	John Player Team Lotus	Lotus 95T-Renault EF4	*lost brake fluid-spun off*

1985

ret	BRAZILIAN GP	Rio	07/04/85	Canon Williams Honda Team	Williams FW10-Honda RA 163-E	*exhaust/accident damage*
5	PORTUGUESE GP	Estoril	21/04/85	Canon Williams Honda Team	Williams FW10-Honda RA 163-E	
5	SAN MARINO GP	Imola	05/05/85	Canon Williams Honda Team	Williams FW10-Honda RA 163-E	
7	MONACO GP	Monte Carlo	19/05/85	Canon Williams Honda Team	Williams FW10-Honda RA 163-E	
6	CANADIAN GP	Montreal	16/06/85	Canon Williams Honda Team	Williams FW10-Honda RA 163-E	
ret	US GP (DETROIT)	Detroit	23/06/85	Canon Williams Honda Team	Williams FW10-Honda RA 163-E	*brake problems-crashed*
dns	FRENCH GP	Paul Ricard	08/07/85	Canon Williams Honda Team	Williams FW10-Honda RA 163-E	*accident in practice*
ret	BRITISH GP	Silverstone	21/07/85	Canon Williams Honda Team	Williams FW10-Honda RA 163-E	*clutch*
6	GERMAN GP	Nürburgring	04/08/85	Canon Williams Honda Team	Williams FW10-Honda RA 163-E	
ret	AUSTRIAN GP	Österreichring	18/08/85	Canon Williams Honda Team	Williams FW10-Honda RA 163-E	*engine*
6	DUTCH GP	Zandvoort	25/08/85	Canon Williams Honda Team	Williams FW10-Honda RA 163-E	
11/*ret*	ITALIAN GP	Monza	08/09/85	Canon Williams Honda Team	Williams FW10-Honda RA 163-E	*engine/Fastest lap*
2	BELGIAN GP	Spa	15/09/85	Canon Williams Honda Team	Williams FW10-Honda RA 163-E	
1	EUROPEAN GP	Brands Hatch	06/10/85	Canon Williams Honda Team	Williams FW10-Honda RA 163-E	
1	SOUTH AFRICAN GP	Kyalami	19/10/85	Canon Williams Honda Team	Williams FW10-Honda RA 163-E	*Pole*
ret	AUSTRALIAN GP	Adelaide	03/11/85	Canon Williams Honda Team	Williams FW10-Honda RA 163-E	*transmission*

1986

ret	BRAZILIAN GP	Rio	23/03/86	Canon Williams Honda Team	Williams FW11-Honda RA 166-E	*accident with Senna*
2	SPANISH GP	Jerez	13/04/86	Canon Williams Honda Team	Williams FW11-Honda RA 166-E	*Fastest lap*
ret	SAN MARINO GP	Imola	27/04/86	Canon Williams Honda Team	Williams FW11-Honda RA 166-E	*engine*
4	MONACO GP	Monte Carlo	11/05/86	Canon Williams Honda Team	Williams FW11-Honda RA 166-E	
1	BELGIAN GP	Spa	25/05/86	Canon Williams Honda Team	Williams FW11-Honda RA 166-E	
1	CANADIAN GP	Montreal	15/06/86	Canon Williams Honda Team	Williams FW11-Honda RA 166-E	*Pole*
5	US GP (DETROIT)	Detroit	22/06/86	Canon Williams Honda Team	Williams FW11-Honda RA 166-E	
1	FRENCH GP	Paul Ricard	06/07/86	Canon Williams Honda Team	Williams FW11-Honda RA 166-E	*Fastest lap*
1	BRITISH GP	Brands Hatch	13/07/86	Canon Williams Honda Team	Williams FW11-Honda RA 166-E	*Fastest lap*
3	GERMAN GP	Hockenheim	27/07/86	Canon Williams Honda Team	Williams FW11-Honda RA 166-E	
3	HUNGARIAN GP	Hungaroring	10/08/86	Canon Williams Honda Team	Williams FW11-Honda RA 166-E	
ret	AUSTRIAN GP	Österreichring	17/08/86	Canon Williams Honda Team	Williams FW11-Honda RA 166-E	*driveshaft*
2	ITALIAN GP	Monza	07/09/86	Canon Williams Honda Team	Williams FW11-Honda RA 166-E	
1	PORTUGUESE GP	Estoril	21/09/86	Canon Williams Honda Team	Williams FW11-Honda RA 166-E	*Fastest lap*
5	MEXICAN GP	Mexico City	12/10/86	Canon Williams Honda Team	Williams FW11-Honda RA 166-E	
ret	AUSTRALIAN GP	Adelaide	26/10/86	Canon Williams Honda Team	Williams FW11-Honda RA 166-E	*tyre failure-crashed/Pole*

1987

6	BRAZILIAN GP	Rio	12/04/87	Canon Williams Honda Team	Williams FW11B-Honda RA 166-E	*Pole*
1	SAN MARINO GP	Imola	03/05/87	Canon Williams Honda Team	Williams FW11B-Honda RA 167-G	
ret	BELGIAN GP	Spa	17/05/87	Canon Williams Honda Team	Williams FW11B-Honda RA 167-G	*accident with Senna/Pole*
ret	MONACO GP	Monte Carlo	31/05/87	Canon Williams Honda Team	Williams FW11B-Honda RA 167-G	*wastegate pipe/Pole*
5	US GP (DETROIT)	Detroit	21/06/87	Canon Williams Honda Team	Williams FW11B-Honda RA 167-G	*Pole*
1	FRENCH GP	Paul Ricard	06/07/87	Canon Williams Honda Team	Williams FW11B-Honda RA 167-G	
1	BRITISH GP	Silverstone	12/07/87	Canon Williams Honda Team	Williams FW11B-Honda RA 167-G	*Fastest lap*
ret	GERMAN GP	Hockenheim	26/07/87	Canon Williams Honda Team	Williams FW11B-Honda RA 167-G	*engine/Pole/Fastest lap*
14/ret	HUNGARIAN GP	Hungaroring	09/08/87	Canon Williams Honda Team	Williams FW11B-Honda RA 167-G	*lost wheel nut/Pole*
1	AUSTRIAN GP	Österreichring	16/08/87	Canon Williams Honda Team	Williams FW11B-Honda RA 167-G	*Fastest lap*
3	ITALIAN GP	Monza	06/08/87	Canon Williams Honda Team	Williams FW11B-Honda RA 167-G	
ret	PORTUGUESE GP	Estoril	21/09/87	Canon Williams Honda Team	Williams FW11B-Honda RA 167-G	*electrics*
1	SPANISH GP	Jerez	27/09/87	Canon Williams Honda Team	Williams FW11B-Honda RA 167-G	
1	MEXICAN GP	Mexico City	18/10/87	Canon Williams Honda Team	Williams FW11B-Honda RA 167-G	*Pole*
dns	JAPANESE GP	Suzuka	01/11/87	Canon Williams Honda Team	Williams FW11B-Honda RA 167-G	*accident in practice*

1988

ret	BRAZILIAN GP	Rio	03/04/88	Canon Williams Team	Williams FW12-Judd CV	*overheating*
ret	SAN MARINO GP	Imola	01/05/88	Canon Williams Team	Williams FW12-Judd CV	*electrics/engine*
ret	MONACO GP	Monte Carlo	15/05/88	Canon Williams Team	Williams FW12-Judd CV	*accident with Alboreto*
ret	MEXICAN GP	Mexico City	29/05/88	Canon Williams Team	Williams FW12-Judd CV	*engine*
ret	CANADIAN GP	Montreal	12/06/88	Canon Williams Team	Williams FW12-Judd CV	*engine*
ret	US GP (DETROIT)	Detroit	19/06/88	Canon Williams Team	Williams FW12-Judd CV	*electrics*
ret	FRENCH GP	Paul Ricard	03/07/88	Canon Williams Team	Williams FW12-Judd CV	*suspension*
2	BRITISH GP	Silverstone	10/07/88	Canon Williams Team	Williams FW12-Judd CV	*Fastest lap*
ret	GERMAN GP	Hockenheim	24/07/88	Canon Williams Team	Williams FW12-Judd CV	*spun off*
ret	HUNGARIAN GP	Hungaroring	07/08/88	Canon Williams Team	Williams FW12-Judd CV	*driver exhaustion*
ret	PORTUGUESE GP	Estoril	25/09/88	Canon Williams Team	Williams FW12-Judd CV	*spun off*
2	SPANISH GP	Jerez	02/10/88	Canon Williams Team	Williams FW12-Judd CV	
ret	JAPANESE GP	Suzuka	30/10/88	Canon Williams Team	Williams FW12-Judd CV	*spun off*
ret	AUSTRALIAN GP	Adelaide	13/11/88	Canon Williams Team	Williams FW12-Judd CV	*brakes/spun off*

1989

1	BRAZILIAN GP	Rio	26/03/89	Scuderia Ferrari SpA SEFAC	Ferrari F1/89	
ret	SAN MARINO GP	Imola	23/04/89	Scuderia Ferrari SpA SEFAC	Ferrari F1/89	
ret	MONACO GP	Monte Carlo	07/05/89	Scuderia Ferrari SpA SEFAC	Ferrari F1/89	*gearbox*
ret	MEXICAN GP	Mexico City	28/05/89	Scuderia Ferrari SpA SEFAC	Ferrari F1/89	*gearbox*
ret	US GP	Phoenix	04/06/89	Scuderia Ferrari SpA SEFAC	Ferrari F1/89	*gearbox/Fastest lap*
dsq	CANADIAN GP	Montreal	18/06/89	Scuderia Ferrari SpA SEFAC	Ferrari F1/89	*gearbox*
2	FRENCH GP	Paul Ricard	09/07/89	Scuderia Ferrari SpA SEFAC	Ferrari F1/89	*black-flagged*
2	BRITISH GP	Silverstone	16/07/89	Scuderia Ferrari SpA SEFAC	Ferrari F1/89	*Fastest lap*

Please note that the results given for the period 1976-80 may be incomplete.

Formula 1 World Championship positions/points (1981-88 inclusive)

1981	14th	8	1985	6th	31
1982	14th	7	1986	2nd	72
1983	12th=	10	1987	2nd	61
1984	9th=	13	1988	10th	12
					214

Formula 1 World Championship placings 1st – 6th + Pole + Fastest laps (From Austria 1980 until Britain 1989 inclusive)

1st	*2nd*	*3rd*	*4th*	*5th*	*6th*	*Pole*	*Fastest lap*
14	7	8	5	5	8	12	12